Freight Forward: Innovative Management Solutions for Manufacturing Logistics

CJ Fernandes

©2024 CJ Fernandes
All Rights Reserved
ISBN: 9798344777191

Published by Fairfords Logistics Ltd
London, United Kingdom

Cover Photo by Wolfgang Weiser

Table of Contents

Chapter 1: Introduction to Manufacturing Logistics 15

The Importance of Logistics in Manufacturing 15

Overview of Supply Chain Optimization 17

Chapter 2: Supply Chain Optimization for Manufacturing 19

Key Principles of Supply Chain Optimization 19

Tools and Technologies for Optimization 21

Case Studies in Successful Optimization 23

Chapter 3: Warehouse Management Systems for Manufacturing 27

Understanding Warehouse Management Systems (WMS) 27

Features of Effective WMS 29

Integrating WMS with Manufacturing Processes 31

Chapter 4: Automation in Manufacturing Logistics 33

The Role of Automation in Logistics 33

Types of Automation Technologies 35

Benefits and Challenges of Automation 37

Chapter 5: Sustainable Logistics Practices in Manufacturing 39

Importance of Sustainability in Logistics 39

Strategies for Sustainable Practices 41

Measuring Sustainability Success 43

Chapter 6: Freight Management Solutions for Manufacturing 47

Overview of Freight Management 47

Choosing the Right Freight Management Solutions 49

Impact of Freight Management on Bottom Line 51

Chapter 7: Cross-Docking Strategies for Efficient Manufacturing 53

    What is Cross-Docking? 53
    Benefits of Cross-Docking in Manufacturing 55
    Implementing Cross-Docking Effectively 57

Chapter 8: Risk Management in Manufacturing Logistics 59

    Identifying Risks in Manufacturing Logistics 59
    Strategies for Mitigating Risks 61
    Developing a Risk Response Plan 63

Chapter 9: Last-Mile Delivery Solutions for Manufacturing Products 65

    Significance of Last-Mile Delivery 65
    Challenges in Last-Mile Delivery 67
    Innovative Solutions for Last-Mile Delivery 69

Chapter 10: Future Trends in Manufacturing Logistics 71

    Emerging Technologies Impacting Logistics 71
    The Shift Towards Digital Logistics 73
    Predictions for the Future of Manufacturing Logistics 75

Chapter 11: Conclusion and Action Plan 77

    Key Takeaways from Each Chapter 77
    Developing a Personalized Action Plan 79
    Moving Forward in Manufacturing Logistics 81

Chapter 1: Introduction to Manufacturing Logistics

The Importance of Logistics in Manufacturing

The role of logistics in manufacturing is integral to operational success and efficiency. Manufacturers are increasingly recognizing the importance of a well-structured logistics framework that aligns with their production processes. Effective logistics management enables manufacturers to optimize their supply chains, ensuring that materials and products move seamlessly from suppliers to production facilities and ultimately to customers. By focusing on logistics, organizations can reduce lead times, lower transportation costs, and enhance overall productivity, which is vital in a competitive market landscape.

Supply chain optimization is a crucial aspect of logistics in manufacturing. It involves the strategic coordination of various operations, including procurement, production, and distribution. For manufacturing leaders, understanding the nuances of supply chain dynamics allows for better forecasting and inventory management, which are essential for maintaining production schedules and meeting customer demand. By leveraging advanced technologies such as Warehouse Management Systems (WMS) and data analytics, manufacturers can gain insights into their supply chains, identify bottlenecks, and implement solutions that drive efficiency.

Automation in manufacturing logistics is another key element that underscores its importance. Automated systems can streamline processes such as order fulfillment, inventory tracking, and transportation management. Implementing automation reduces human error, accelerates processing times, and enhances accuracy in logistics operations. As manufacturers adopt robotics and artificial intelligence, they can also achieve greater flexibility in their logistics strategies, adapting quickly to changes in market demand or production requirements, thus maintaining a competitive edge.

Sustainable logistics practices have emerged as a priority for manufacturers looking to minimize their environmental impact. By incorporating sustainable transportation methods, optimizing route planning, and utilizing eco-friendly packaging, manufacturers can not only reduce their carbon footprint but also appeal to environmentally conscious consumers. Sustainable logistics not only contributes to corporate social responsibility but can also result in cost savings and improved brand reputation, making it a strategic consideration for manufacturing leaders.

Finally, effective risk management in manufacturing logistics is essential for navigating the uncertainties of the supply chain. Manufacturers face various risks, including supply disruptions, regulatory changes, and fluctuating market conditions. By developing robust logistics strategies that incorporate risk assessment and contingency planning, manufacturers can mitigate potential disruptions that may affect production or delivery. Furthermore, last-mile delivery solutions play a critical role in ensuring that finished products reach their final destination efficiently, addressing customer expectations for timeliness and reliability. By prioritizing logistics, manufacturing leaders can create resilient operations capable of thriving in an ever-evolving landscape.

Overview of Supply Chain Optimization

Supply chain optimization is a critical aspect for manufacturing leaders seeking to enhance efficiency, reduce costs, and improve service levels. At its core, supply chain optimization involves the strategic alignment of various components within the supply chain, including procurement, production, inventory management, and distribution. By analyzing and refining these interconnected processes, manufacturers can achieve a streamlined operation that responds effectively to market demands while minimizing waste and maximizing resource utilization. The integration of advanced technologies and data analytics plays a pivotal role in identifying bottlenecks and inefficiencies, allowing businesses to implement targeted improvements.

One of the key elements of supply chain optimization is the implementation of advanced warehouse management systems (WMS). These systems facilitate real-time inventory tracking, order fulfillment, and space utilization, significantly enhancing operational efficiency. A well-designed WMS can reduce cycle times and improve accuracy in order processing, which is vital for maintaining customer satisfaction. Moreover, the integration of automation technologies within the warehouse environment further enhances productivity by minimizing manual tasks and reducing the likelihood of errors. As manufacturing leaders explore these technologies, they can expect substantial gains in throughput and reliability.

Automation in manufacturing logistics is not only about enhancing warehouse operations; it also extends to the entire supply chain. Automated solutions, such as robotic process automation (RPA) and artificial intelligence (AI), can optimize various logistics functions, including transportation planning and inventory replenishment. By leveraging these technologies, manufacturers can achieve greater agility, allowing them to respond swiftly to changes in demand or supply disruptions. Furthermore, the adoption of automation can lead to significant cost savings by reducing labor costs and improving accuracy in forecasting and demand planning.

Sustainable logistics practices have become increasingly important in supply chain optimization. With growing awareness of environmental impacts, manufacturers are now seeking ways to implement more sustainable practices throughout their logistics operations. This includes optimizing transportation routes to reduce emissions, utilizing eco-friendly packaging materials, and adopting energy-efficient warehouse designs. By embracing sustainability, manufacturing leaders not only enhance their corporate social responsibility profile but also improve operational efficiency and potentially reduce costs in the long term.

Finally, effective risk management strategies are essential for optimizing supply chains in manufacturing. The unpredictable nature of global markets, combined with potential disruptions from natural disasters, geopolitical tensions, or supplier failures, necessitates a proactive approach to identifying and mitigating risks. By employing robust risk management frameworks, manufacturers can enhance their resilience and ensure continuity in operations. This includes developing contingency plans, diversifying supplier bases, and utilizing technology to monitor and respond to potential threats. A comprehensive approach to risk management not only safeguards the supply chain but also supports overall optimization efforts by fostering a more secure and reliable logistics environment.

Chapter 2: Supply Chain Optimization for Manufacturing

Key Principles of Supply Chain Optimization

Key principles of supply chain optimization play a crucial role in enhancing manufacturing logistics, ensuring that processes are efficient, cost-effective, and sustainable. Understanding these principles enables manufacturing leaders to streamline operations, reduce waste, and respond more effectively to market demands. The core tenets include visibility, collaboration, automation, sustainability, and risk management. Each of these elements contributes to a more resilient supply chain capable of adapting to changing circumstances.

Visibility is fundamental in supply chain optimization, as it allows manufacturers to track inventory levels, monitor production processes, and assess supplier performance in real time. By implementing advanced warehouse management systems, organizations gain insights into their logistics operations, enabling proactive decision-making. Enhanced visibility not only facilitates better inventory management but also supports timely responses to disruptions, ensuring that manufacturing operations remain agile and efficient.

Collaboration among all stakeholders in the supply chain is essential for creating a seamless flow of information and resources. Manufacturers should foster partnerships with suppliers, logistics providers, and customers to share data and align objectives. This collaborative approach helps in identifying bottlenecks, optimizing routes, and improving communication across the supply chain. By working together, organizations can leverage collective strengths, resulting in a more integrated and responsive logistics network.

Automation is another key principle that significantly impacts supply chain optimization. By integrating automation technologies, such as robotics and artificial intelligence, manufacturers can enhance productivity and reduce operational costs. Automated systems streamline processes such as inventory management, order fulfillment, and transportation planning, minimizing human error and increasing efficiency. Embracing automation leads to faster response times and allows for more strategic allocation of resources within manufacturing logistics.

Sustainability is increasingly becoming a priority for manufacturers, and incorporating sustainable logistics practices is vital for long-term success. By optimizing transportation routes, reducing packaging waste, and implementing energy-efficient warehouse operations, manufacturers can significantly decrease their environmental footprint. Moreover, sustainable practices can enhance brand reputation and fulfill consumer demand for eco-friendly products. Finally, effective risk management strategies must be integrated into supply chain optimization to mitigate potential disruptions. Identifying vulnerabilities, developing contingency plans, and continuously monitoring risks ensure that manufacturers can maintain operations even in the face of unexpected challenges, ultimately leading to a more resilient supply chain.

Tools and Technologies for Optimization

In the realm of manufacturing logistics, optimization is crucial for enhancing efficiency and reducing costs. Several tools and technologies have emerged that facilitate this optimization, allowing manufacturers to streamline their supply chain processes effectively. These innovations encompass various aspects of logistics, including warehouse management systems (WMS), automation solutions, and freight management systems. By leveraging these technologies, manufacturers can achieve significant improvements in their operational performance, thereby fostering growth and competitiveness in the market.

Warehouse Management Systems play a pivotal role in optimizing inventory control and order fulfillment processes. Modern WMS offer real-time visibility into inventory levels, allowing manufacturers to make informed decisions about stock replenishment and allocation. These systems integrate seamlessly with other supply chain technologies, providing a comprehensive view of warehouse operations. By automating routine tasks such as picking, packing, and shipping, WMS not only reduce labor costs but also minimize errors, leading to enhanced customer satisfaction. Manufacturers that adopt advanced WMS can significantly improve their order accuracy and turnaround times, which are essential to meeting the demands of today's fast-paced market.

Automation has become a cornerstone of modern manufacturing logistics, driving efficiency and precision in various processes. Automated guided vehicles (AGVs), robotic process automation (RPA), and smart conveyors are just a few examples of how automation technologies are transforming logistics operations. These tools reduce the reliance on manual labor, mitigate the risk of human error, and enhance the speed of operations. Furthermore, automation allows for better space utilization within warehouses, as automated systems can operate in tighter spaces and handle complex workflows. Manufacturers that embrace automation not only improve their operational efficiency but also position themselves to respond quickly to changing market conditions.

Sustainable logistics practices are increasingly becoming a priority for manufacturers seeking to enhance their environmental responsibility. Technologies that enable energy-efficient transportation, such as route optimization software and electric vehicles, contribute to reducing the carbon footprint of logistics operations. Additionally, sustainable packaging solutions and waste reduction initiatives play a significant role in optimizing the supply chain. By incorporating sustainability into their logistics strategies, manufacturers can not only comply with regulatory requirements but also appeal to environmentally conscious consumers. This shift towards sustainable practices can lead to cost savings and improved brand reputation in the long run.

Lastly, effective risk management strategies are essential for navigating the complexities of manufacturing logistics. Advanced analytics and predictive modeling tools enable manufacturers to identify potential disruptions in the supply chain and develop contingency plans accordingly. Technologies such as blockchain can enhance traceability and transparency, allowing manufacturers to monitor their supply chains in real-time. By implementing robust risk management solutions, manufacturers can reduce vulnerabilities and ensure continuity in their logistics operations. A proactive approach to risk management not only safeguards against potential losses but also strengthens the overall resilience of the manufacturing supply chain.

Case Studies in Successful Optimization

In the realm of manufacturing logistics, successful optimization can profoundly impact efficiency, profitability, and sustainability. This subchapter explores exemplary case studies that highlight innovative strategies and practical solutions across various niches. These real-world examples serve as a testament to how manufacturing leaders can implement changes that lead to significant improvements in their operations.

One notable case is that of a mid-sized electronics manufacturer that adopted an advanced Warehouse Management System (WMS). By integrating real-time inventory tracking and automated picking solutions, the company reduced order fulfillment times by 30%. This optimization not only improved customer satisfaction but also lowered labor costs. The implementation of data analytics within the WMS enabled managers to predict inventory needs more accurately, thus minimizing overstock and stockouts. The lessons learned from this case underline the critical role of technology in enhancing warehouse operations and the importance of aligning system capabilities with business goals.

Another compelling example involves a large beverage manufacturer that sought to streamline its supply chain through automation. By introducing robotics in its distribution centers, the company achieved a 40% increase in order processing speed while simultaneously reducing errors. This strategic move allowed the manufacturer to adapt quickly to fluctuating market demands and improve overall service levels. Furthermore, the organization invested in training its workforce to work alongside automated systems, ensuring that employees could leverage technology effectively. This case highlights the transformative potential of automation in manufacturing logistics and the necessity of workforce adaptability.

Sustainable logistics practices have also shown promising results in optimization. A furniture manufacturer implemented a circular supply chain model, focusing on waste reduction and resource efficiency. By redesigning packaging and utilizing recyclable materials, the company not only reduced its environmental footprint but also cut transportation costs by 15%. The adoption of sustainable practices resonated well with consumers, leading to increased brand loyalty and sales. This case illustrates how integrating sustainability into logistics can yield both environmental benefits and financial gains, positioning manufacturers as leaders in responsible production.

Lastly, a case study on a global automotive manufacturer illustrates the effectiveness of cross-docking strategies. By reorganizing its distribution network to prioritize cross-docking, the company minimized storage times and improved inventory turnover. This approach allowed for quicker movement of goods from inbound to outbound shipping, resulting in a 25% reduction in operating costs. Additionally, the manufacturer established strong relationships with its suppliers to ensure timely deliveries, further enhancing efficiency. This case underscores the importance of collaboration and strategic planning in achieving operational excellence within manufacturing logistics.

These case studies exemplify successful optimization strategies across various facets of manufacturing logistics. By learning from these examples, manufacturing owners and leaders can identify opportunities for improvement and implement innovative solutions that drive efficiency, sustainability, and profitability in their operations.

Chapter 3: Warehouse Management Systems for Manufacturing

Understanding Warehouse Management Systems (WMS)

Understanding Warehouse Management Systems (WMS) is crucial for manufacturing leaders aiming to optimize supply chain operations. A WMS is a sophisticated software solution designed to facilitate and streamline warehouse functionalities. It provides real-time visibility into inventory levels and locations, enabling manufacturers to manage stock more effectively. By automating processes such as receiving, picking, packing, and shipping, WMS minimizes human error and enhances operational efficiency. This leads to improved accuracy in order fulfillment and can significantly reduce lead times, which is essential in today's fast-paced market.

Incorporating a WMS into manufacturing logistics allows for better inventory control and tracking. This system uses barcoding or RFID technology to monitor goods throughout the warehouse. As items move through various stages, the WMS updates inventory counts in real-time, ensuring that manufacturers always have accurate data regarding stock levels. This capability is particularly beneficial in avoiding stockouts or overstock situations, both of which can disrupt production schedules and impact customer satisfaction. Furthermore, effective inventory management contributes to sustainable logistics practices by reducing waste and optimizing resource utilization.

Automation is a key aspect of modern warehouse management, and WMS plays a pivotal role in this transition. With features that support automated guided vehicles (AGVs), robotic picking systems, and conveyor systems, manufacturers can enhance their operational capabilities. Automation not only accelerates warehouse processes but also reduces labor costs and improves workplace safety. By integrating WMS with other automation technologies, manufacturers can achieve a seamless flow of information and materials, resulting in a more responsive supply chain that can adapt to changing demands.

Cross-docking strategies are another critical area where a WMS proves advantageous. This method involves unloading materials from incoming trucks and directly loading them onto outbound trucks, minimizing storage time and reducing handling costs. A robust WMS facilitates this process by providing detailed scheduling and tracking capabilities, ensuring that shipments are processed quickly and accurately. By optimizing cross-docking operations, manufacturers can enhance their distribution efficiency, reduce inventory holding costs, and improve overall customer service.

Lastly, the implementation of a WMS can significantly mitigate risks in manufacturing logistics. By offering comprehensive data analytics and reporting features, a WMS enables manufacturers to identify potential bottlenecks and inefficiencies in their processes. This insight allows for proactive decision-making and risk management strategies that can avert disruptions in the supply chain. Furthermore, with enhanced visibility into the logistics network, manufacturers can better manage last-mile delivery solutions, ensuring that products reach their destinations on time and in optimal condition. By embracing Warehouse Management Systems, manufacturing leaders position themselves for sustained success in an increasingly competitive landscape.

Features of Effective WMS

An effective Warehouse Management System (WMS) is essential for manufacturing operations aiming to enhance efficiency and reduce costs. One of the key features of a robust WMS is real-time inventory tracking. This capability allows manufacturers to monitor stock levels continuously, leading to improved accuracy in inventory management. By utilizing barcode scanning and RFID technology, businesses can ensure that they have the right materials available at the right time, minimizing the risk of production delays due to stockouts or excess inventory. Real-time tracking also facilitates better forecasting and planning, which are crucial for maintaining a responsive supply chain.

Another significant feature of an effective WMS is its ability to integrate seamlessly with other systems used in manufacturing logistics. This interoperability streamlines operations by ensuring that data flows smoothly between the WMS, ERP systems, and transportation management software. Such integration enhances visibility across the supply chain, enabling manufacturers to make informed decisions based on comprehensive data analysis. Additionally, it supports automation initiatives, allowing for processes such as order picking, packing, and shipping to be executed with minimal human intervention, thereby increasing productivity and reducing the likelihood of errors.

Automation is a critical component of modern WMS solutions, and effective systems leverage technology to optimize warehouse operations. Automated processes such as robotic picking systems, automated guided vehicles, and smart shelving can significantly increase throughput while reducing labor costs. By implementing such technologies, manufacturers can achieve faster order fulfillment and improve overall operational efficiency. Furthermore, advanced WMS platforms utilize machine learning algorithms to optimize picking routes and inventory placement, enhancing the speed and accuracy of warehouse operations.

Scalability is another vital feature of an effective WMS, particularly for manufacturing businesses that anticipate growth or fluctuations in demand. A scalable WMS can easily adapt to changes in inventory volume, product variety, and operational complexity. This flexibility ensures that manufacturers can respond promptly to market demands without requiring a complete system overhaul. As businesses expand or diversify their product lines, a scalable WMS can support these changes by providing the necessary tools and functionalities to manage increased complexity in logistics and warehouse operations.

Lastly, sustainable logistics practices are becoming increasingly important within manufacturing, and an effective WMS can play a pivotal role in supporting these initiatives. Features such as energy-efficient warehouse layouts, waste reduction strategies, and a focus on minimizing transportation emissions can be integrated into the WMS. By optimizing routes and reducing unnecessary movements within the warehouse, manufacturers can lower their carbon footprint while also improving their overall efficiency. As organizations strive to embrace sustainability, a WMS that supports these goals helps not only in compliance with regulations but also in enhancing the company's reputation and customer loyalty in a market that values environmental responsibility.

Integrating WMS with Manufacturing Processes

Integrating Warehouse Management Systems (WMS) with manufacturing processes is a critical strategy for manufacturers aiming to optimize their supply chain and enhance operational efficiency. The synergy between WMS and manufacturing operations facilitates real-time inventory tracking, streamlined production schedules, and improved order fulfillment. By aligning these two vital components, manufacturers can ensure that materials are available when needed, minimizing downtime and maximizing productivity. A seamless integration allows for better communication across departments, thereby enhancing decision-making and fostering a culture of collaboration.

One of the primary benefits of integrating WMS with manufacturing processes is the visibility it provides throughout the supply chain. With real-time data on inventory levels, production status, and shipment tracking, manufacturers can make informed decisions that enhance responsiveness to market demands. This visibility helps in identifying bottlenecks and inefficiencies within the production line, allowing companies to implement corrective measures swiftly. By leveraging advanced analytics, manufacturers can predict trends, optimize inventory levels, and reduce waste, leading to a more sustainable operational model.

Automation plays a crucial role in the integration of WMS and manufacturing processes. Automated systems can facilitate the transfer of information between the warehouse and the production floor, ensuring that all stakeholders have access to the same data. For instance, automated inventory replenishment can trigger production orders based on real-time stock levels, thereby preventing shortages and excess inventory. In addition, automation reduces manual errors, enhances speed, and improves accuracy in both warehousing and manufacturing operations. This not only leads to cost savings but also increases overall customer satisfaction through timely delivery of products.

Sustainable logistics practices are increasingly becoming a focal point for manufacturers. Integrating WMS with manufacturing processes enables companies to adopt more environmentally friendly practices throughout their operations. For example, by optimizing transportation routes and reducing idle times through synchronized manufacturing and warehousing activities, manufacturers can lower their carbon footprint. Furthermore, an integrated system can facilitate recycling and waste management initiatives by providing insights into material flow and usage, ultimately promoting a circular economy within the manufacturing sector.

Lastly, effective risk management is essential for maintaining stability in manufacturing logistics. Integrating WMS with manufacturing processes allows for better identification and mitigation of risks associated with supply chain disruptions. By having access to accurate, real-time data, manufacturers can develop contingency plans and respond swiftly to unexpected events, such as supplier delays or sudden changes in demand. This proactive approach not only safeguards production timelines but also enhances the resilience of the supply chain, ensuring that manufacturers can navigate challenges while maintaining operational continuity.

Chapter 4: Automation in Manufacturing Logistics

The Role of Automation in Logistics

The role of automation in logistics has become increasingly vital for manufacturing leaders aiming to enhance efficiency and reduce operational costs. Automation technologies, such as robotics, artificial intelligence, and advanced software systems, facilitate the seamless integration of various logistical processes. For manufacturing companies, implementing these technologies can lead to improved inventory management, streamlined operations, and enhanced accuracy in order fulfillment. As a result, manufacturers can respond more swiftly to market demands while minimizing errors and delays that can disrupt the supply chain.

Warehouse management systems (WMS) play a crucial role in automating logistics processes. These systems enable real-time tracking of inventory levels, optimizing storage solutions, and improving order picking accuracy. By automating these tasks, manufacturers can increase throughput and reduce the time spent on manual inventory checks and stock replenishment. Moreover, advanced WMS solutions often incorporate data analytics, allowing manufacturers to forecast demand more effectively and make informed decisions about inventory levels, ultimately contributing to supply chain optimization.

In the realm of transportation, automation streamlines freight management solutions by utilizing technologies such as transportation management systems (TMS) and route optimization software. These tools facilitate better planning and execution of shipping processes, from selecting carriers to tracking shipments in real-time. By automating these logistics functions, manufacturing leaders can enhance visibility across the supply chain, reduce transportation costs, and improve delivery times. This efficiency not only benefits the manufacturer but also enhances customer satisfaction by ensuring timely and accurate deliveries.

Sustainable logistics practices are also significantly impacted by automation. Automated systems can optimize routes and consolidate shipments, resulting in reduced fuel consumption and lower carbon emissions. Additionally, by employing smart technologies, manufacturers can analyze their logistics operations to identify areas for sustainability improvements. This focus on automation not only aligns with environmental goals but can also lead to cost savings, making it a strategic priority for modern manufacturing entities committed to responsible practices.

Finally, the last-mile delivery solutions in manufacturing logistics are increasingly benefiting from automation. The advent of automated delivery vehicles and drones presents new opportunities for efficient and cost-effective delivery methods. These innovations help manufacturers address the challenges of last-mile logistics, particularly in urban areas where congestion can impede timely delivery. By embracing automation in this critical segment of the supply chain, manufacturing leaders can enhance their service offerings and bolster their competitiveness in the market.

Types of Automation Technologies

Automation technologies in manufacturing logistics can be categorized into several distinct types, each offering unique benefits that can enhance operational efficiency, reduce costs, and improve overall supply chain performance. These technologies range from basic mechanization to advanced robotics and artificial intelligence systems. Understanding these types enables manufacturing leaders to make informed decisions about which solutions best align with their operational goals and sustainability initiatives.

One prominent type of automation technology is robotic process automation (RPA). RPA utilizes software robots to automate repetitive tasks usually performed by human workers. In manufacturing logistics, this can include data entry, inventory management, and order processing. By implementing RPA, manufacturers can minimize errors, speed up operations, and free up human resources for more strategic tasks, ultimately leading to improved productivity and better resource allocation.

Another significant category is warehouse automation systems, which incorporate technologies like automated guided vehicles (AGVs), conveyor systems, and automated storage and retrieval systems (AS/RS). These systems streamline warehouse operations by optimizing the movement of goods and reducing the time spent on manual handling. With the increasing complexity of supply chains, warehouse automation plays a crucial role in enhancing accuracy and efficiency, enabling manufacturers to meet the demands of just-in-time production and rapid order fulfillment.

Artificial intelligence (AI) and machine learning are also transformative automation technologies in manufacturing logistics. By analyzing vast amounts of data, these technologies can predict trends, optimize inventory levels, and enhance demand forecasting. AI-driven analytics can provide insights that lead to more informed decision-making, allowing manufacturers to adapt to market changes swiftly and efficiently. Moreover, AI can facilitate dynamic routing for last-mile delivery solutions, ensuring that products reach their destinations in a timely and cost-effective manner.

Lastly, the Internet of Things (IoT) is revolutionizing how manufacturers manage their logistics operations. IoT devices can monitor equipment performance, track shipments in real-time, and provide valuable insights into supply chain conditions. This connectivity allows for proactive maintenance of machinery, reducing downtime and risks associated with equipment failure. Additionally, IoT can enhance sustainability practices by optimizing resource usage and minimizing waste, aligning with modern manufacturing's emphasis on environmentally responsible operations.

In conclusion, the various types of automation technologies available to manufacturing leaders can significantly impact supply chain optimization and logistics efficiency. By leveraging robotic process automation, warehouse automation systems, artificial intelligence, and the Internet of Things, manufacturers can improve operational performance, enhance decision-making, and achieve sustainable logistics practices. As the landscape of manufacturing logistics continues to evolve, embracing these technologies will be essential for maintaining a competitive edge and meeting the increasing demands of the market.

Benefits and Challenges of Automation

Automation in manufacturing logistics presents a myriad of benefits that can significantly enhance operational efficiency and productivity. One of the primary advantages is the reduction in labor costs. By implementing automated systems, manufacturers can minimize the reliance on manual labor for repetitive tasks, allowing human resources to focus on more strategic activities. This shift not only reduces expenses but also leads to increased output, as machines can operate continuously without the need for breaks or downtime. Furthermore, automation contributes to improved accuracy in processes, reducing the likelihood of human error and ensuring consistent quality in manufacturing outputs.

Another critical benefit of automation is enhanced supply chain visibility and control. With advanced technologies such as Internet of Things (IoT) devices and real-time data analytics, manufacturers can track inventory levels, monitor production processes, and manage logistics operations more effectively. This increased visibility allows for better decision-making, enabling manufacturers to respond swiftly to changes in demand or disruptions in the supply chain. Additionally, automation facilitates improved communication among stakeholders, leading to more streamlined operations and collaboration across the supply chain.

Despite these advantages, the integration of automation in manufacturing logistics comes with its own set of challenges. One significant concern is the initial investment required for automation technology. Many manufacturing leaders may hesitate to allocate substantial resources toward upgrading their systems, particularly if they are uncertain about the return on investment. Furthermore, the complexity of implementing new technologies can lead to operational disruptions, as staff may require training to adapt to automated processes. This transition period can strain existing resources and may temporarily impact productivity levels.

Another challenge associated with automation is the potential impact on the workforce. While automation can lead to job displacement in certain roles, it can also create opportunities for new positions that focus on managing and maintaining automated systems. Manufacturers must navigate this delicate balance by providing retraining and upskilling programs for existing employees. Emphasizing a culture of adaptability and continuous learning is essential for ensuring that the workforce evolves alongside technological advancements, fostering an environment where human expertise complements automated solutions.

Finally, manufacturers must consider the long-term sustainability of their automated systems. While automation can lead to increased efficiency and reduced waste, it is crucial to implement these solutions in a way that aligns with sustainable logistics practices. This involves selecting technologies that minimize energy consumption and environmental impact. Additionally, manufacturers should regularly evaluate their automated processes to ensure they continue to meet sustainability goals while adapting to changing market demands. By addressing these challenges, manufacturers can fully leverage the benefits of automation, positioning themselves for success in a rapidly evolving logistics landscape.

Chapter 5: Sustainable Logistics Practices in Manufacturing

Importance of Sustainability in Logistics

Sustainability in logistics has become a critical component for manufacturing businesses aiming to enhance their operational efficiency while minimizing environmental impact. As supply chains grow increasingly complex, the emphasis on sustainable practices not only helps in reducing the carbon footprint but also leads to cost savings and improved brand reputation. For manufacturing leaders, integrating sustainability into logistics operations is no longer optional; it is essential for long-term viability and competitiveness in the marketplace. By prioritizing sustainable logistics practices, manufacturers can optimize their supply chains, streamline warehouse management, and enhance overall operational resilience.

Implementing sustainable logistics practices in manufacturing can significantly improve supply chain optimization. By analyzing transportation routes, choosing fuel-efficient modes of transportation, and consolidating shipments, manufacturers can reduce energy consumption and emissions. This approach not only aligns with environmental goals but also leads to reduced logistics costs. Furthermore, optimizing supply chains through sustainability can foster stronger relationships with suppliers and customers, who increasingly value eco-friendly operations. In this context, sustainability becomes a strategic advantage that enhances operational efficiency while addressing the growing demand for corporate responsibility.

Warehouse management systems play a vital role in promoting sustainability within logistics. Advanced technologies enable manufacturers to monitor inventory levels in real-time, reducing waste and improving space utilization. By employing automated systems that incorporate sustainability metrics, organizations can better manage resources and minimize excess inventory. This not only leads to cost reductions but also supports sustainable practices by reducing the environmental impact associated with overproduction and storage. Efficient warehouse management, therefore, becomes a crucial element in the broader strategy of sustainable logistics.

Automation in manufacturing logistics also contributes to sustainability efforts by increasing efficiency and minimizing human error. Automated systems can optimize route planning for transportation, ensuring that goods are delivered in the most efficient manner possible. This not only reduces fuel consumption but also enhances delivery times and customer satisfaction. Moreover, automation facilitates better data collection and analysis, allowing manufacturers to identify areas for improvement and implement sustainable practices across their operations. As such, embracing automation is pivotal for manufacturing leaders looking to enhance their logistics operations sustainably.

Finally, effective risk management in logistics is intertwined with sustainability initiatives. By assessing potential risks associated with environmental regulations, supply chain disruptions, and changing consumer preferences, manufacturers can develop robust strategies that mitigate these challenges. Sustainable logistics practices, such as cross-docking and efficient last-mile delivery solutions, enable manufacturers to respond swiftly to market changes while maintaining a focus on sustainability. This proactive approach not only safeguards against potential risks but also positions manufacturing leaders as responsible stewards of their supply chains, fostering trust and loyalty among customers and stakeholders. In conclusion, the importance of sustainability in logistics is paramount for manufacturing businesses striving for innovation and efficiency in their operations.

Strategies for Sustainable Practices

In the realm of manufacturing logistics, the adoption of sustainable practices is essential for long-term viability and competitiveness. Strategies for sustainable practices not only contribute to environmental stewardship but also enhance operational efficiency and reduce costs. To begin, manufacturers should conduct a thorough assessment of their supply chains, identifying key areas where sustainability can be integrated. This includes evaluating the sourcing of materials, energy consumption, and waste management processes. By recognizing and addressing these areas, manufacturers can develop targeted strategies that align with their sustainability goals while optimizing supply chain performance.

One effective strategy is the implementation of advanced warehouse management systems (WMS) that prioritize sustainability. These systems can optimize inventory management, reduce energy consumption through smart lighting and climate control, and streamline operations to minimize waste. Utilizing data analytics, manufacturers can forecast demand more accurately, reducing excess inventory and its associated carrying costs. Furthermore, integrating automation within warehouses can enhance efficiency, minimize human error, and reduce the carbon footprint associated with manual processes, leading to a more sustainable operation overall.

In the context of freight management, adopting a multimodal approach can significantly enhance sustainability. By leveraging various transportation methods, manufacturers can select the most efficient and environmentally friendly options for their supply chains. This may involve using rail for long-distance transportation and trucks for last-mile delivery, thereby reducing fuel consumption and emissions. Additionally, implementing cross-docking strategies can eliminate unnecessary handling and storage, further minimizing the environmental impact of logistics operations. These strategies not only lower costs but also contribute to a more sustainable supply chain.

Risk management is another vital aspect of implementing sustainable practices in manufacturing logistics. By identifying potential risks associated with environmental regulations, supply chain disruptions, and resource scarcity, manufacturers can develop proactive strategies to mitigate these risks. Incorporating sustainability into risk management frameworks ensures that organizations are prepared for changes in regulations and market demand, allowing for a smoother transition to sustainable practices. This foresight not only protects the business but also enhances its reputation as a socially responsible entity.

Finally, engaging in continuous improvement and employee training programs focused on sustainability can foster a culture of environmental responsibility within manufacturing organizations. Encouraging employees to participate in sustainability initiatives, from waste reduction programs to energy-saving campaigns, can lead to innovative solutions and a more committed workforce. As manufacturers embrace these strategies for sustainable practices, they position themselves not only as leaders in the industry but also as stewards of the environment, paving the way for a more sustainable future in manufacturing logistics.

Measuring Sustainability Success

Measuring sustainability success in manufacturing logistics requires a comprehensive approach that integrates various metrics and methodologies. For manufacturing leaders, understanding how to assess sustainability efforts is crucial for continuous improvement and long-term viability. Key performance indicators (KPIs) such as carbon footprint reduction, waste minimization, and resource efficiency are foundational metrics that should be monitored. By establishing baseline measurements, manufacturers can track progress over time and adjust strategies as necessary to enhance sustainability outcomes. This data-driven approach ensures that sustainability initiatives align with overall business objectives.

One effective method for measuring sustainability success is the use of life cycle assessments (LCAs). LCAs provide a holistic view of the environmental impact of products from raw material extraction through production, distribution, use, and disposal. By analyzing each phase of the product life cycle, manufacturers can identify areas where they can reduce emissions, optimize resource use, and minimize waste. Implementing LCAs enables manufacturers to make informed decisions about material selection, production processes, and logistics strategies, ultimately leading to more sustainable practices across the supply chain.

Another critical aspect of measuring sustainability success is the incorporation of technology and data analytics in warehouse management systems and automation processes. Advanced technologies such as the Internet of Things (IoT) and artificial intelligence (AI) can provide real-time data on energy consumption, transportation efficiency, and inventory turnover rates. By leveraging these analytics, manufacturers can pinpoint inefficiencies and implement targeted improvements. Automation can also reduce human error and enhance accuracy, further contributing to sustainability by minimizing waste and optimizing resource allocation.

In addition to internal metrics, external certifications and benchmarks play a significant role in measuring sustainability success. Certifications such as ISO 14001 for environmental management and LEED for green building can provide third-party validation of sustainability efforts. Participating in industry benchmarks allows manufacturers to compare their performance against peers and identify best practices. This competitive analysis not only fosters a culture of continuous improvement but also enhances brand reputation, as consumers increasingly favor companies with strong sustainability credentials.

Lastly, engaging stakeholders in the measurement process is essential for fostering a culture of sustainability within manufacturing organizations. Employees, suppliers, and customers can provide valuable insights into sustainability practices and their effectiveness. Regular communication and collaboration with these stakeholders facilitate the sharing of knowledge and best practices, creating a robust framework for sustainability measurement. By creating partnerships focused on sustainability, manufacturers can drive collective action that leads to more significant achievements in sustainability success and a stronger, more resilient supply chain.

Chapter 6: Freight Management Solutions for Manufacturing

Overview of Freight Management

Freight management is a critical component of the supply chain that directly impacts the efficiency and profitability of manufacturing operations. It encompasses the planning, execution, and monitoring of the movement of goods from the point of origin to the final destination. For manufacturing leaders, understanding the nuances of freight management is essential to optimize costs, streamline processes, and enhance overall supply chain performance. By effectively managing freight, manufacturers can ensure that products reach customers on time, reduce lead times, and improve service levels.

One vital aspect of freight management is the selection of appropriate transportation modes and carriers. Manufacturers must evaluate various options such as road, rail, air, and sea freight, taking into account factors like cost, transit time, and reliability. The choice of carrier can significantly influence delivery performance and customer satisfaction. Moreover, utilizing technologies such as transportation management systems (TMS) allows manufacturers to analyze data, track shipments, and make informed decisions regarding freight routing and carrier selection, thereby optimizing their logistics operations.

Incorporating automation into freight management processes can enhance efficiency and reduce human error. Automation tools can facilitate the generation of shipping documents, track inventory levels, and manage order fulfillment processes. By integrating warehouse management systems (WMS) with freight management solutions, manufacturers can create a seamless flow of information that enhances visibility across the supply chain. This integration not only improves operational efficiency but also enables better coordination between various stakeholders, including suppliers, carriers, and customers.

Sustainable logistics practices are increasingly becoming a priority for manufacturers seeking to minimize their environmental footprint. Freight management plays a crucial role in this effort, as optimizing transportation routes and consolidating shipments can lead to reduced fuel consumption and lower emissions. Manufacturers should consider engaging with carriers that prioritize sustainability, such as those using alternative fuel vehicles or implementing energy-efficient practices. By adopting sustainable freight management strategies, manufacturers can not only comply with regulations but also enhance their brand reputation and appeal to environmentally conscious consumers.

Lastly, effective risk management strategies are essential in freight management to mitigate potential disruptions in the supply chain. Manufacturers must assess risks such as transportation delays, regulatory changes, and geopolitical factors that could impact freight operations. Implementing robust contingency plans and diversifying transportation options can help manufacturers navigate uncertainties. Additionally, leveraging data analytics can provide insights into potential risks, enabling proactive decision-making. By prioritizing risk management within freight management practices, manufacturers can ensure greater resilience and adaptability in their logistics operations.

Choosing the Right Freight Management Solutions

Choosing the right freight management solutions is a critical decision for manufacturing leaders aiming to optimize their supply chains. With the increasing complexity of logistics and the demands of modern consumers, manufacturers must consider solutions that not only enhance efficiency but also align with their operational goals. A well-chosen freight management system can streamline processes, reduce costs, and improve service delivery, making it essential to evaluate various options carefully. Key factors to consider include the integration capabilities of the solution, user-friendliness, scalability, and the ability to provide real-time visibility into shipments.

Integration with existing systems is paramount when selecting a freight management solution. Many manufacturers already utilize various software tools for warehouse management, order processing, and inventory control. Therefore, a solution that can seamlessly connect with these systems will enhance overall operational efficiency and minimize disruptions. Moreover, manufacturers should prioritize solutions that support automation, as this can significantly reduce manual tasks, decrease errors, and free up valuable resources for more strategic activities. Automation features, such as automatic shipment tracking and reporting, can lead to more informed decision-making and quicker response times.

Scalability is another crucial consideration. As manufacturing operations grow, the freight management solution should be capable of adapting to increased volumes and changing logistics needs. A flexible system allows manufacturers to adjust their logistics strategies without the need for a complete overhaul of their technology infrastructure. Furthermore, as global trade continues to evolve, the ability to manage multiple carriers, modes of transport, and international regulations becomes increasingly important. Solutions that offer robust scalability will enable manufacturers to stay competitive in dynamic markets.

Sustainability is becoming a vital aspect of logistics management, especially for manufacturers looking to enhance their brand image and meet regulatory requirements. Freight management solutions that incorporate sustainable practices can help reduce carbon footprints and optimize routes to minimize fuel consumption. By choosing solutions that provide insights into environmental impacts and facilitate eco-friendly shipping options, manufacturers can demonstrate their commitment to sustainability while also potentially lowering costs through more efficient operations.

Lastly, effective risk management features within freight management solutions are essential for mitigating potential disruptions in the supply chain. Manufacturers face various risks, including fluctuating fuel prices, regulatory changes, and unforeseen events like natural disasters. A robust freight management system should provide tools for assessing risks, developing contingency plans, and ensuring compliance with industry regulations. By prioritizing risk management, manufacturers can safeguard their operations and maintain continuity, ultimately leading to greater resilience in their logistics processes.

Impact of Freight Management on Bottom Line

Effective freight management plays a crucial role in determining the profitability and overall financial health of manufacturing operations. By optimizing freight processes, manufacturers can significantly reduce transportation costs, enhance supply chain efficiency, and improve service delivery to clients. This proactive approach not only streamlines logistics but also positions manufacturing entities to respond swiftly to market demands. Consequently, a well-structured freight management system can translate into substantial savings and increased revenues, driving a positive impact on the bottom line.

One of the primary ways freight management affects the bottom line is through cost reduction. By employing strategies such as route optimization and load consolidation, manufacturers can minimize shipping expenses. Advanced warehouse management systems enable accurate inventory tracking and forecasting, which further aids in reducing unnecessary freight costs associated with overstocking or stockouts. Moreover, leveraging automation in logistics processes can help eliminate human errors, leading to fewer costly delays and disruptions. As a result, manufacturers can allocate resources more effectively, enhancing overall operational efficiency.

Sustainable logistics practices are becoming increasingly important in the manufacturing sector, not only for environmental compliance but also for cost savings. Implementing eco-friendly freight management solutions can lead to reduced fuel consumption and lower carbon emissions, which often equates to financial incentives and tax breaks. Additionally, adopting sustainable practices can enhance a company's brand image and appeal to environmentally conscious consumers, thus potentially increasing market share. By integrating sustainability into freight management, manufacturers can achieve dual benefits of cost savings and improved reputation, ultimately benefitting their bottom line.

Cross-docking strategies represent another critical aspect of freight management that influences profitability. By minimizing storage time and expediting the movement of goods from inbound to outbound transportation, manufacturers can enhance delivery speed and reduce handling costs. Efficient cross-docking practices can lead to shorter lead times and improved cash flow, as products move quickly through the supply chain. This agility allows manufacturers to respond to customer demands more effectively, fostering customer loyalty and repeat business, which are essential for maintaining a healthy bottom line.

Finally, risk management in freight operations cannot be overlooked, as it directly impacts financial performance. By identifying potential risks in the supply chain, such as disruptions in transportation or fluctuations in fuel prices, manufacturers can develop contingency plans and strategies to mitigate these risks. Implementing robust risk management practices not only protects against unforeseen challenges but also ensures consistent service delivery, thereby maintaining customer satisfaction. A reliable freight management system that incorporates risk assessment can safeguard profits by minimizing the financial impact of disruptions, thereby solidifying its role in enhancing the bottom line for manufacturing enterprises.

Chapter 7: Cross-Docking Strategies for Efficient Manufacturing

What is Cross-Docking?

Cross-docking is a logistics practice that streamlines the supply chain by reducing storage time and increasing efficiency. In this process, products are directly transferred from inbound transportation to outbound transportation, eliminating the need for long-term storage in warehouses. For manufacturing owners and leaders, understanding cross-docking is essential as it can significantly enhance operational efficiency, minimize handling costs, and speed up the delivery process. By consolidating shipments, manufacturers can respond more quickly to customer demands and improve overall service levels.

The mechanics of cross-docking involve the receipt of goods in a facility, where they are sorted and immediately prepared for outbound shipment to customers or retail locations. This practice is particularly beneficial for manufacturers with high-volume and time-sensitive products, as it allows for a quick turnover of inventory. By leveraging cross-docking, manufacturers can reduce the amount of warehouse space needed, thus lowering overhead costs and optimizing resource utilization within the supply chain.

Incorporating cross-docking into a manufacturing logistics strategy requires a well-coordinated warehouse management system. This system must be capable of efficiently managing the flow of goods, tracking inventory levels, and coordinating with transportation providers. Automation plays a vital role in this process, as automated systems can facilitate real-time data exchange, streamline operations, and minimize human error. By implementing advanced technologies, manufacturers can ensure that the cross-docking process is seamless and enhances overall productivity.

Sustainable logistics practices can also benefit from cross-docking, as this method reduces the carbon footprint associated with warehousing and handling. By minimizing the time products spend in transit and decreasing the need for storage, manufacturers can contribute to a more sustainable supply chain model. This approach not only meets the growing demand for environmentally friendly practices but also demonstrates a commitment to corporate social responsibility, which can enhance brand reputation and customer loyalty.

Lastly, effective risk management in cross-docking operations is crucial for mitigating potential disruptions in the supply chain. Manufacturers must develop contingency plans to address unexpected delays or disruptions in transportation. By maintaining flexibility in their logistics strategies and utilizing data analytics, manufacturers can better anticipate and respond to risks, ensuring that their cross-docking operations remain efficient and effective. By embracing cross-docking, manufacturing leaders can achieve a competitive edge in their industries, driving both operational excellence and customer satisfaction.

Benefits of Cross-Docking in Manufacturing

Cross-docking is a logistics strategy that has gained significant traction in the manufacturing sector due to its ability to streamline operations and enhance supply chain efficiency. By minimizing the handling and storage of goods, cross-docking enables manufacturers to reduce lead times and lower inventory costs. This method allows for a more agile response to market demands, as products can be quickly transferred from inbound to outbound transportation without the need for extensive warehousing. As a result, manufacturers can maintain a leaner inventory, which is crucial in today's fast-paced market environment.

One of the primary benefits of cross-docking in manufacturing is improved operational efficiency. By consolidating incoming shipments and directly transferring them to outgoing transport, manufacturers can significantly decrease the time goods spend in transit. This not only accelerates delivery times but also reduces the labor and resources needed for handling and storage. With fewer dock-to-stock processes, manufacturers can optimize their workforce and automate various aspects of logistics, leading to enhanced productivity and cost savings.

Moreover, cross-docking contributes to sustainable logistics practices, which are increasingly important for modern manufacturers. By reducing the need for extensive warehousing, cross-docking minimizes the energy consumption associated with storing and handling products. This approach also decreases the overall carbon footprint of logistics operations, aligning with the growing emphasis on sustainability in manufacturing. Implementing cross-docking can enhance a company's reputation as an environmentally responsible entity, which can be a significant competitive advantage in a market where consumers increasingly prefer sustainable products.

In addition to operational and environmental benefits, cross-docking also plays a critical role in risk management within manufacturing logistics. By minimizing the time products spend in transit and storage, manufacturers can reduce the risk of inventory obsolescence and damage. Furthermore, cross-docking supports more effective inventory management strategies by ensuring that products are moved efficiently based on real-time demand rather than being held in stock for extended periods. This proactive approach to inventory can help manufacturers quickly adapt to fluctuations in demand, thereby mitigating risks associated with overproduction and excess inventory.

Finally, cross-docking enhances last-mile delivery solutions in manufacturing by optimizing the flow of goods from distribution centers to end customers. With a focus on speed and efficiency, manufacturers can ensure that products reach customers in a timely manner, improving service levels and customer satisfaction. As manufacturers increasingly rely on advanced warehouse management systems and automation technologies, the integration of cross-docking strategies becomes essential. This combination not only supports efficient logistics operations but also positions manufacturers to respond to evolving market demands and customer expectations, ultimately driving business growth and success.

Implementing Cross-Docking Effectively

Implementing cross-docking effectively requires a strategic approach that aligns with the overall objectives of the manufacturing supply chain. One of the first steps is to assess the current warehouse layout and transportation processes. A well-organized facility facilitates the smooth transfer of goods from inbound to outbound shipments. Manufacturers should evaluate their existing systems, identifying bottlenecks and inefficiencies that could hinder cross-docking operations. This assessment should include a thorough analysis of inventory levels, product flow, and the capabilities of existing personnel and equipment. Streamlining these elements lays the foundation for a successful cross-docking strategy.

Next, technology plays a crucial role in optimizing cross-docking operations. Integrating advanced warehouse management systems (WMS) can enhance real-time visibility and control over inventory movements. These systems can automate order processing, track shipments, and provide data analytics to inform decision-making. Additionally, utilizing automated guided vehicles (AGVs) and conveyor systems can significantly reduce the time required to move goods through the cross-docking area. By investing in the right technologies, manufacturers can improve efficiency, minimize handling costs, and enhance the accuracy of inventory management.

Training and engaging staff is equally important for successful cross-docking implementation. Employees must understand the principles of cross-docking and their specific roles within the process. Regular training sessions can help familiarize staff with new technologies and processes, ensuring they are equipped to handle the demands of a fast-paced environment. Moreover, fostering a culture of continuous improvement encourages workers to identify challenges and suggest solutions, which can lead to further efficiencies and innovations within the cross-docking framework.

Collaboration with transportation partners is vital to the success of cross-docking strategies. Manufacturers should establish strong relationships with carriers and logistics providers to ensure timely deliveries and pickups. Effective communication channels can facilitate better coordination between inbound and outbound shipments, reducing dwell times and improving overall service levels. Additionally, leveraging data sharing and visibility tools can enhance collaboration, allowing all parties to respond proactively to any disruptions or changes in demand.

Finally, monitoring and evaluating the performance of cross-docking operations is essential for sustained success. Key performance indicators (KPIs) such as turnaround times, order accuracy, and cost savings should be established to measure effectiveness. Regularly reviewing these metrics allows manufacturers to identify areas for improvement and adapt their strategies accordingly. By maintaining a focus on continuous improvement and adapting to market changes, manufacturers can ensure that their cross-docking operations remain efficient, responsive, and aligned with their overall supply chain objectives.

Chapter 8: Risk Management in Manufacturing Logistics

Identifying Risks in Manufacturing Logistics

Identifying risks in manufacturing logistics is crucial for ensuring operational efficiency and maintaining competitive advantage. The complexity of supply chains, combined with the dynamic nature of global markets, introduces various potential risks that can disrupt manufacturing operations. These risks can stem from multiple sources, including supplier reliability, transportation disruptions, regulatory compliance, and technological failures. By systematically identifying and assessing these risks, manufacturing leaders can implement proactive strategies to mitigate their impact and ensure continuity in logistics operations.

One of the primary areas of risk is the supply chain itself, where disruptions can occur due to unforeseen events such as natural disasters, geopolitical tensions, or supplier insolvencies. Manufacturing leaders must conduct thorough risk assessments of their suppliers, evaluating their financial stability, operational capabilities, and contingency plans. This proactive approach enables manufacturers to diversify their supplier base and avoid reliance on single sources, thereby enhancing resilience in their supply chains. Additionally, establishing strong relationships with suppliers can facilitate better communication and quicker responses to potential issues.

Transportation risks also play a significant role in manufacturing logistics. Delays in shipping, accidents, and fluctuating fuel costs can all hinder timely product delivery. To address these risks, manufacturers should analyze transportation routes and modes, leveraging data analytics to identify potential bottlenecks and optimize logistics operations. Implementing advanced tracking technologies can further enhance visibility across the supply chain, allowing for real-time monitoring and quicker adjustments in response to disruptions. By fostering a robust transportation strategy, manufacturers can minimize delays and maintain consistent delivery schedules.

Regulatory compliance poses another critical risk in manufacturing logistics. With varying regulations across regions and industries, manufacturers must stay informed about compliance requirements related to safety, environmental standards, and labor laws. Non-compliance can lead to significant fines, product recalls, and reputational damage. To mitigate these risks, manufacturers should invest in compliance management systems that keep track of relevant regulations and ensure adherence. Regular training for employees and open communication channels can also aid in fostering a culture of compliance within the organization.

Lastly, the integration of automation in manufacturing logistics introduces both opportunities and risks. While automation can streamline operations and reduce human error, it also presents challenges such as system failures and cybersecurity threats. Manufacturing leaders must assess the technology they implement, ensuring that robust security measures are in place to protect sensitive data and operational integrity. Furthermore, ongoing maintenance and employee training are essential for maximizing the benefits of automated systems while minimizing associated risks. By proactively addressing these potential challenges, manufacturers can harness the power of automation to enhance logistics efficiency and drive sustainable growth.

Strategies for Mitigating Risks

In the realm of manufacturing logistics, mitigating risks is essential for maintaining operational efficiency and ensuring the resilience of supply chains. Manufacturing owners and leaders must adopt a multifaceted approach to risk management that encompasses various strategies tailored to their specific niches. Understanding the unique challenges faced within supply chain optimization, warehouse management systems, and automation is crucial. By implementing proactive measures, organizations can safeguard against potential disruptions and enhance their overall logistics performance.

One effective strategy for mitigating risks involves the integration of advanced technology into warehouse management systems. By leveraging real-time data analytics and inventory management solutions, manufacturers can gain better visibility into their supply chain operations. This visibility allows for improved forecasting, helping to anticipate demand fluctuations and avoid stockouts or overstock situations. Furthermore, automation technologies streamline processes, reduce human error, and enhance operational efficiency, thereby minimizing the risks associated with manual handling and inefficiencies in logistics.

Sustainable logistics practices also play a pivotal role in risk mitigation. As consumers and regulatory bodies increasingly demand environmentally responsible operations, manufacturers must adapt their logistics strategies accordingly. Implementing eco-friendly practices not only helps in reducing carbon footprints but also mitigates risks related to compliance and reputational damage. Strategies such as optimizing transportation routes to reduce emissions, adopting energy-efficient warehousing solutions, and utilizing sustainable packaging materials can significantly enhance a company's resilience and public perception.

In addition to technological and sustainable strategies, manufacturers should consider cross-docking techniques to further mitigate risks associated with inventory management and transportation. By facilitating the direct transfer of goods from inbound to outbound transportation, cross-docking minimizes storage time and reduces handling costs. This approach can significantly enhance the speed and efficiency of last-mile delivery solutions, ensuring that products reach customers promptly. The reduction in inventory holding also decreases the risk of obsolescence and associated financial losses.

Finally, a comprehensive risk management framework must include regular assessment and adaptation to emerging threats. This involves conducting risk assessments to identify vulnerabilities within the supply chain, such as geopolitical factors, natural disasters, or market fluctuations. By establishing contingency plans and fostering collaborative relationships with suppliers and logistics partners, manufacturers can enhance their ability to respond swiftly to unforeseen challenges. Emphasizing a culture of continuous improvement in risk management practices will not only protect manufacturing operations but also provide a competitive edge in an increasingly complex logistics landscape.

Developing a Risk Response Plan

Developing a Risk Response Plan is a critical step for manufacturing leaders aiming to safeguard their operations against potential disruptions. In the context of supply chain optimization, it is imperative to identify potential risks that could impact production schedules, inventory levels, and overall efficiency. This involves a thorough assessment of both internal and external factors, such as supply chain vulnerabilities, equipment failures, regulatory changes, and market fluctuations. By understanding the landscape of risks, manufacturing owners can prioritize those that pose the greatest threat to their operations and take proactive measures.

Once the risks have been identified, the next stage is to devise appropriate response strategies. These strategies can be categorized into four main types: avoidance, mitigation, transfer, and acceptance. Avoidance involves altering plans to sidestep risks entirely. For example, a manufacturing facility might diversify its supplier base to reduce dependence on a single source. Mitigation strategies, on the other hand, aim to reduce the impact or likelihood of risks. Implementing advanced warehouse management systems can enhance inventory accuracy and reduce stockouts, thereby diminishing the risk of operational delays.

Risk transfer is another effective strategy, often accomplished through insurance or outsourcing certain operations. Manufacturing leaders may choose to partner with third-party logistics providers who can manage specific aspects of the supply chain, thus transferring some risks associated with transportation and logistics. Acceptance acknowledges the inherent risks in manufacturing but requires a clear understanding of the potential consequences and a plan for managing them if they materialize. This approach is often suitable for low-probability, high-impact risks where the cost of mitigation may outweigh the potential losses.

In developing a comprehensive risk response plan, it is essential to involve key stakeholders across the organization. This collaborative approach ensures that all perspectives are considered, and it fosters a culture of risk awareness. Regular workshops and training sessions can be organized to educate employees about potential risks and the importance of adhering to the established response strategies. By creating a team-oriented environment, manufacturing leaders can enhance the effectiveness of their risk management efforts and ensure that everyone is prepared to act in the event of a disruption.

Finally, manufacturing leaders must recognize that a risk response plan is not static; it should be continually reviewed and updated based on evolving market conditions, technological advancements, and lessons learned from past experiences. Regular audits and scenario planning exercises can help identify gaps in the existing plan and determine new risks that may arise. By maintaining a proactive stance toward risk management, manufacturing organizations can enhance their resilience, streamline their operations, and ultimately drive sustainable growth in an increasingly complex logistics environment.

Chapter 9: Last-Mile Delivery Solutions for Manufacturing Products

Significance of Last-Mile Delivery

Last-mile delivery represents a crucial component in the logistics chain, particularly for manufacturing enterprises looking to optimize their supply chain. This phase of the delivery process encompasses the final leg of transportation, where products are delivered from a distribution center to the end customer. For manufacturing leaders, ensuring efficiency in last-mile delivery not only impacts customer satisfaction but also directly influences operational costs and overall competitiveness. Understanding the significance of this segment enables manufacturers to make informed decisions that enhance service levels while minimizing expenses.

The efficiency of last-mile delivery can significantly affect inventory management and warehouse operations. Delays or inefficiencies in this stage can lead to excess inventory, which ties up capital and increases storage costs. By implementing advanced warehouse management systems, manufacturers can track inventory levels in real-time, improving demand forecasting and reducing lead times. This synchronization between last-mile delivery and warehouse management allows for better resource allocation, ensuring that products are available when and where they are needed, thus maintaining a seamless flow throughout the supply chain.

Sustainable logistics practices are becoming increasingly important in manufacturing logistics, and last-mile delivery is no exception. Manufacturers are under growing pressure to reduce their environmental footprint, and optimizing last-mile logistics can be a significant contributor to this goal. By adopting eco-friendly transportation methods, utilizing electric vehicles, or implementing efficient route planning technologies, manufacturers can reduce emissions and promote sustainability. This approach not only aligns with corporate social responsibility initiatives but can also enhance brand reputation and customer loyalty as consumers become more environmentally conscious.

The integration of automation in last-mile delivery solutions is transforming how manufacturers approach logistics. Automated systems, such as drones and robotic delivery vehicles, are being explored to improve delivery speed and reduce labor costs. These technologies enable manufacturers to overcome traditional delivery challenges, enhancing reliability and efficiency. By investing in automation, manufacturing leaders can streamline operations, reduce human error, and improve overall service quality, thereby meeting the increasing demands of their customers for faster and more reliable deliveries.

Moreover, effective risk management strategies are essential for mitigating the uncertainties associated with last-mile delivery. Disruptions can arise from various sources, including traffic congestion, adverse weather conditions, or unexpected demand spikes. By developing comprehensive risk management frameworks, manufacturers can identify potential vulnerabilities in their last-mile operations and implement contingency plans. This proactive approach not only safeguards against potential losses but also ensures that manufacturers can maintain service continuity, reinforcing customer trust and loyalty in an increasingly competitive market.

Challenges in Last-Mile Delivery

Last-mile delivery represents one of the most complex challenges in the logistics landscape, particularly for manufacturing firms striving for efficiency and customer satisfaction. This final leg of the supply chain often involves unique hurdles that can significantly impact overall operational performance. Factors such as geographic constraints, urban congestion, and varying customer expectations create a multifaceted environment where traditional logistics strategies may fall short. Manufacturing leaders must recognize these challenges and develop comprehensive approaches to navigate them effectively.

One of the primary challenges in last-mile delivery is the unpredictability of urban environments. As cities continue to grow, the complexity of delivering products within them increases. Traffic congestion, limited access points, and varying regulations can lead to delays and increased transportation costs. Manufacturers must invest in route optimization technologies and real-time tracking systems to enhance their delivery processes. By leveraging data analytics, companies can better anticipate traffic patterns and adjust delivery schedules, thereby minimizing disruptions and improving service reliability.

Customer expectations are also evolving, with consumers increasingly demanding faster and more flexible delivery options. In the context of manufacturing, this presents a significant challenge, as the production and delivery timelines must be carefully coordinated. Manufacturers must adopt agile supply chain practices that allow for quicker response times while maintaining product quality. Implementing innovative delivery solutions, such as on-demand transportation and localized distribution centers, can help address these shifting expectations and enhance customer satisfaction.

Sustainability is another critical consideration in last-mile delivery for manufacturers. As environmental concerns grow, companies are under pressure to reduce their carbon footprints and adopt greener practices. This includes optimizing delivery routes to minimize vehicle emissions and exploring alternative delivery methods, such as electric vehicles or bicycle couriers. Embracing sustainable logistics practices not only meets regulatory demands but also appeals to environmentally conscious consumers, thereby adding value to the brand and enhancing competitiveness in the market.

Finally, risk management in last-mile delivery cannot be overlooked. The final leg of the supply chain is fraught with potential disruptions, from weather-related delays to unforeseen logistical challenges. Manufacturers must develop robust risk management strategies that identify potential vulnerabilities and implement mitigation plans. This may involve diversifying delivery partners, investing in insurance coverage, or utilizing technology to gain visibility into the supply chain. By proactively addressing these risks, manufacturing leaders can ensure greater resilience and adaptability in their last-mile delivery operations, ultimately contributing to long-term success.

Innovative Solutions for Last-Mile Delivery

Last-mile delivery represents a critical juncture in the supply chain, particularly for manufacturers striving to enhance customer satisfaction while maintaining operational efficiency. Traditional delivery methods often face challenges such as rising costs, inefficiencies, and increased consumer expectations for rapid service. Innovative solutions are essential to address these challenges and optimize last-mile delivery processes. By leveraging technology and adopting creative strategies, manufacturers can ensure timely and efficient product distribution, ultimately translating to improved customer loyalty and competitive advantage.

One promising approach to enhancing last-mile delivery is the integration of advanced tracking systems. Utilizing real-time GPS and IoT (Internet of Things) technologies allows manufacturers to monitor their shipments at every stage of the delivery process. This transparency not only improves operational efficiency by enabling prompt adjustments to delivery routes and schedules but also fosters trust among customers who appreciate visibility into the status of their orders. Furthermore, data analytics can provide valuable insights into delivery patterns, allowing firms to refine their logistics strategies for better performance.

Collaboration with local delivery services and crowd-sourced logistics platforms is another innovative strategy that manufacturers can adopt. By partnering with these services, manufacturers can leverage existing local knowledge and infrastructure, reducing delivery times and costs. This model also allows for greater flexibility in scaling operations, as businesses can adapt their delivery capacities based on demand fluctuations without the need for significant investment in their own logistics resources. Such collaborations can lead to more sustainable delivery practices by minimizing empty miles and optimizing load capacities.

Automation is transforming last-mile delivery, with solutions such as autonomous vehicles and drones now becoming viable options for manufacturers. These technologies can significantly reduce labor costs and improve delivery speed, especially in urban areas where traffic congestion is prevalent. While regulatory and technical challenges remain, the potential for increased efficiency and reduced carbon footprints makes the exploration of these automated solutions worthwhile. Manufacturers must stay informed about advancements in this area to remain competitive and innovative in their delivery operations.

Lastly, adopting sustainable logistics practices in last-mile delivery can enhance a manufacturer's brand image while meeting the growing consumer demand for environmentally friendly practices. Implementing electric vehicles, optimizing delivery routes to reduce emissions, and utilizing eco-friendly packaging are all steps that contribute to a more sustainable approach. By prioritizing sustainability in their last-mile delivery strategies, manufacturers not only comply with regulatory requirements but also appeal to environmentally conscious customers, thereby positioning themselves favorably in a competitive market. Embracing these innovative solutions will be pivotal for manufacturers aiming to excel in the evolving landscape of logistics and supply chain management.

Chapter 10: Future Trends in Manufacturing Logistics

Emerging Technologies Impacting Logistics

Emerging technologies are revolutionizing the logistics landscape, particularly in manufacturing. As manufacturers strive for efficiency and competitiveness, they are increasingly adopting innovations that streamline operations, reduce costs, and enhance service levels. Technologies such as the Internet of Things (IoT), artificial intelligence (AI), and blockchain are becoming integral to logistics strategies, allowing for real-time tracking, predictive analytics, and improved supply chain transparency. These advancements not only facilitate better decision-making but also enable manufacturers to respond swiftly to market demands and supply chain disruptions.

The implementation of IoT in logistics allows for unprecedented visibility throughout the supply chain. Sensors and connected devices provide real-time data on inventory levels, equipment status, and environmental conditions. This information is vital for optimizing warehouse management systems, as it enables manufacturers to maintain optimal stock levels, reduce waste, and improve order accuracy. With IoT, manufacturers can monitor their assets in transit, ensuring timely deliveries and enhancing customer satisfaction. This technology also plays a crucial role in predictive maintenance, where data analytics can forecast equipment failures before they occur, minimizing downtime and associated costs.

Artificial intelligence is another transformative technology impacting logistics. AI algorithms can analyze vast amounts of data to identify patterns and trends that inform supply chain optimization. In manufacturing logistics, AI can enhance demand forecasting, enabling more accurate production planning and inventory management. By leveraging machine learning, manufacturers can refine their logistics strategies, automate routine tasks, and improve operational efficiency. Moreover, AI can streamline freight management solutions by optimizing routing and load planning, ultimately reducing shipping costs and transit times.

Blockchain technology is reshaping the logistics sector by providing a secure and transparent method for recording transactions. This decentralized ledger system enhances traceability throughout the supply chain, allowing manufacturers to verify the authenticity of products and track their journey from production to delivery. In the context of sustainable logistics practices, blockchain can facilitate the sharing of data regarding the environmental impact of logistics operations, enabling manufacturers to make informed decisions that align with their sustainability goals. Additionally, it aids in risk management by ensuring that all parties in the supply chain have access to accurate and up-to-date information, reducing the likelihood of disputes.

Lastly, the emergence of advanced last-mile delivery solutions is transforming how manufacturers approach the final leg of the logistics journey. Technologies such as drones and autonomous vehicles are gaining traction, providing efficient alternatives for delivering products directly to customers. These innovations not only expedite delivery times but also enhance customer experience by offering more flexible and reliable options. As manufacturers embrace these technologies, they can better meet consumer expectations while simultaneously reducing transportation costs and environmental footprints. By integrating these emerging technologies into their logistics strategies, manufacturers can significantly enhance their operational capabilities and competitiveness in an increasingly complex market.

The Shift Towards Digital Logistics

The shift towards digital logistics is transforming the way manufacturing leaders approach supply chain management. As technology continues to advance, manufacturers are increasingly adopting digital tools to enhance their logistics operations. This transition is primarily driven by the need for greater efficiency, transparency, and responsiveness within the supply chain. Digital logistics enables manufacturers to streamline processes, reduce costs, and improve service levels, ultimately leading to a more competitive position in the market.

One of the key components of this digital transformation is the implementation of sophisticated warehouse management systems (WMS). These systems provide real-time visibility into inventory levels, order statuses, and warehouse operations. By leveraging data analytics, manufacturers can optimize storage space, improve picking accuracy, and enhance overall warehouse efficiency. This not only leads to reduced operational costs but also facilitates better decision-making and responsiveness to market demands.

Automation is another critical aspect of digital logistics that manufacturers are embracing. Automated systems can handle various logistics functions, from inventory management to order fulfillment, with minimal human intervention. This shift not only increases productivity but also reduces the likelihood of errors associated with manual processes. By integrating automation into their logistics operations, manufacturers can achieve greater scalability, allowing them to respond swiftly to fluctuations in demand and operational challenges.

Sustainable logistics practices are gaining importance in the digital logistics landscape as well. With growing awareness of environmental impacts, manufacturers are increasingly seeking ways to reduce their carbon footprint and enhance sustainability. Digital tools can help optimize transportation routes, reduce waste, and improve energy efficiency throughout the supply chain. By adopting sustainable logistics practices, manufacturers can not only comply with regulations but also appeal to environmentally conscious consumers, thereby enhancing their brand reputation.

Lastly, the development of risk management strategies is essential in navigating the complexities of modern logistics. Digital logistics solutions provide manufacturers with tools to identify potential risks, assess their impact, and implement mitigation strategies. By utilizing advanced analytics and machine learning, manufacturers can anticipate disruptions and develop contingency plans, ensuring continuity in their operations. This proactive approach to risk management is critical in maintaining supply chain resilience and safeguarding the overall health of manufacturing logistics.

Predictions for the Future of Manufacturing Logistics

As the landscape of manufacturing logistics evolves, several predictions emerge that will significantly impact the way manufacturers operate. One of the foremost trends is the increasing integration of advanced technologies into supply chain processes. The adoption of artificial intelligence and machine learning will enhance supply chain optimization, enabling manufacturers to analyze vast amounts of data in real time. This predictive analytics capability will allow businesses to make informed decisions regarding inventory management, demand forecasting, and production scheduling, ultimately improving efficiency and reducing costs.

Warehouse management systems (WMS) are also poised for transformation as manufacturers prioritize agility and responsiveness. Future WMS solutions will likely leverage the Internet of Things (IoT) to provide real-time visibility of inventory levels and location. This will empower manufacturers to implement more effective replenishment strategies and reduce lead times. Furthermore, as e-commerce continues to expand, WMS will need to adapt to accommodate smaller, more frequent shipments, requiring a shift in warehouse layout and operations to facilitate increased throughput and flexibility.

Automation will play a pivotal role in the future of manufacturing logistics. Robotics and automated guided vehicles (AGVs) will become commonplace in warehouses and production facilities, streamlining processes such as picking, packing, and transportation of goods. This shift toward automation will not only enhance operational efficiency but also alleviate labor shortages by reducing the reliance on manual labor. Manufacturers will need to invest in training for their workforce to manage and maintain these automated systems, ensuring a smooth transition and maximizing the return on investment.

Sustainable logistics practices will increasingly dictate the strategies employed by manufacturers. As environmental concerns gain prominence, manufacturers will be compelled to adopt greener supply chain practices. This will include optimizing transportation routes to reduce carbon footprints, utilizing energy-efficient warehousing solutions, and implementing waste reduction initiatives throughout the logistics process. The emphasis on sustainability will not only meet regulatory requirements but also resonate with consumers who prioritize environmentally responsible products, potentially leading to enhanced brand loyalty and market competitiveness.

Lastly, risk management in manufacturing logistics will become more crucial as global uncertainties persist. Manufacturers will need to develop robust contingency plans to address potential disruptions caused by geopolitical tensions, natural disasters, or pandemics. This will involve diversifying suppliers, investing in flexible logistics solutions, and enhancing last-mile delivery capabilities to ensure customer satisfaction. The emphasis on resilience in the supply chain will require leaders to adopt a proactive approach, preparing their organizations to navigate challenges while maintaining operational continuity and fulfilling customer demands.

Chapter 11: Conclusion and Action Plan

Key Takeaways from Each Chapter

In "Freight Forward: Innovative Management Solutions for Manufacturing Logistics," each chapter presents critical insights tailored for manufacturing owners and leaders. The first chapter lays the groundwork by emphasizing the necessity of supply chain optimization. It highlights how an efficient supply chain can significantly enhance productivity and reduce costs. Key takeaways include the importance of real-time data analytics for decision-making and the integration of technology to streamline operations, ensuring that manufacturing processes are agile and responsive to market demands.

The second chapter delves into warehouse management systems (WMS) specifically designed for the manufacturing sector. It outlines how advanced WMS can improve inventory accuracy, reduce lead times, and enhance order fulfillment rates. Readers learn about the benefits of automation in warehouses, such as reduced labor costs and minimized human error. The chapter also stresses the importance of selecting a WMS that aligns with the unique requirements of the manufacturing environment, ensuring seamless integration with existing systems.

Automation in manufacturing logistics is the focus of the third chapter, which emphasizes the transformative impact of automated solutions on operational efficiency. Key takeaways include the role of robotics in handling repetitive tasks, the use of AI for predictive maintenance, and the integration of IoT devices for enhanced visibility across the supply chain. The chapter advocates for a strategic approach to automation, where manufacturers assess their processes to identify areas that would benefit most from technological advancements, ultimately leading to increased productivity and cost-effectiveness.

Sustainable logistics practices are explored in the fourth chapter, where the emphasis is on the growing importance of environmental responsibility in manufacturing logistics. Key takeaways include strategies for reducing carbon footprints through optimized transportation routes, implementing eco-friendly packaging solutions, and adopting renewable energy sources within logistics operations. The chapter encourages manufacturers to view sustainability not just as a regulatory requirement but as a competitive advantage that can enhance brand reputation and customer loyalty.

The final chapter addresses the complexities of risk management in manufacturing logistics, focusing on the need for proactive strategies to mitigate potential disruptions. Key takeaways highlight the importance of developing contingency plans, diversifying supply sources, and investing in technology that provides real-time risk assessments. Additionally, the chapter discusses last-mile delivery solutions tailored for manufacturing products, emphasizing the need for efficient delivery mechanisms to enhance customer satisfaction and drive repeat business. Overall, the book synthesizes these insights into a comprehensive guide that empowers manufacturing leaders to navigate the evolving landscape of logistics effectively.

Developing a Personalized Action Plan

Developing a personalized action plan tailored to the unique needs of a manufacturing business is essential for optimizing logistics and enhancing operational efficiency. This action plan should start with a comprehensive assessment of current logistics processes, including supply chain management, warehouse operations, and freight movements. By identifying bottlenecks, inefficiencies, and areas for improvement, manufacturing leaders can create a baseline from which to develop targeted strategies that align with their specific objectives and operational constraints.

The next step in formulating a personalized action plan involves setting clear, measurable goals. These goals should reflect the overarching vision of the manufacturing operation while considering short-term and long-term objectives. For instance, a company may aim to reduce lead times by 20 percent within six months or increase warehouse space utilization by 15 percent over the next year. Establishing these benchmarks not only provides direction but also facilitates tracking progress and making necessary adjustments along the way.

Incorporating advanced technologies is crucial in the development of an effective action plan. Automation tools, warehouse management systems, and data analytics can significantly enhance manufacturing logistics. By evaluating available technologies and their applicability to specific logistics challenges, manufacturing leaders can select solutions that drive efficiency and reduce costs. This decision-making process should consider factors such as return on investment, ease of integration, and scalability to ensure that the chosen technology aligns with long-term operational goals.

Sustainable logistics practices should also be a key component of the action plan. As environmental concerns gain prominence, manufacturing leaders must consider strategies that minimize their ecological footprint. This can include optimizing transportation routes to reduce emissions, implementing energy-efficient warehouse practices, and exploring eco-friendly packaging options. By committing to sustainability, manufacturers not only enhance their corporate social responsibility but also attract customers who prioritize environmentally conscious practices.

Finally, risk management strategies should be integrated into the personalized action plan. Manufacturing logistics can be susceptible to various risks, including supply chain disruptions, fluctuating demand, and regulatory changes. By identifying potential risks and establishing contingency plans, manufacturing leaders can mitigate the impact of these challenges on operations. Regularly reviewing and updating the action plan in response to evolving circumstances will ensure that the manufacturing operation remains agile and resilient, ultimately leading to sustained success in an increasingly competitive market.

Moving Forward in Manufacturing Logistics

In the rapidly evolving landscape of manufacturing logistics, moving forward requires a keen understanding of supply chain optimization. Manufacturers must prioritize strategies that enhance efficiency and reduce costs while maintaining product quality. Implementing advanced analytics tools can provide insights into inventory levels, production schedules, and demand forecasts. This data-driven approach allows manufacturers to respond proactively to market changes, ensuring that operations remain agile and competitive. By leveraging technologies such as IoT and AI, manufacturers can optimize their supply chains, streamline operations, and ultimately improve customer satisfaction.

Warehouse management systems (WMS) play a critical role in the logistics of manufacturing. A robust WMS can significantly enhance inventory accuracy, reduce lead times, and improve order fulfillment rates. By automating routine processes such as stock tracking and order processing, manufacturers can minimize human error and ensure a smoother workflow. Utilizing real-time data, manufacturers can make informed decisions regarding inventory levels and replenishment strategies. Furthermore, integrating WMS with other systems, such as enterprise resource planning (ERP) software, can create a seamless flow of information across the organization, fostering collaboration and enhancing productivity.

The advent of automation in manufacturing logistics has revolutionized traditional practices. Automated systems can handle repetitive tasks such as picking, packing, and sorting, freeing human resources to focus on more strategic initiatives. Robotics and automated guided vehicles (AGVs) are increasingly being deployed in warehouses and manufacturing floors to improve efficiency and safety. Additionally, automation can lead to significant cost savings by reducing labor costs and minimizing errors. As manufacturers consider automation, it is essential to evaluate the return on investment and the impact on workforce dynamics, ensuring that the transition is both economically viable and socially responsible.

Sustainable logistics practices are becoming increasingly important for manufacturers who aim to reduce their environmental footprint. Implementing green logistics strategies, such as optimizing transportation routes and utilizing energy-efficient equipment, can lead to significant cost savings and enhanced brand reputation. Manufacturers should also consider the sustainability of their supply chain partners, opting for suppliers who prioritize eco-friendly practices. Educating employees about sustainability initiatives fosters a culture of responsibility and innovation, encouraging teams to identify and implement additional sustainable practices throughout the logistics process.

Finally, effective freight management solutions are essential for navigating the complexities of last-mile delivery in manufacturing logistics. This stage of the supply chain often presents challenges due to varying customer locations, delivery timeframes, and transportation costs. Employing advanced freight management software can help manufacturers track shipments in real time, optimize delivery routes, and manage carrier relationships. Additionally, exploring cross-docking strategies can enhance efficiency by reducing handling times and inventory levels, ultimately leading to faster delivery to customers. By addressing these critical areas, manufacturers can position themselves for success in an increasingly competitive market.

Fairfords Logistics Ltd is a UK-based freight forwarding and warehouse management company based in London. The Company helps several industries to move their goods across the globe.

Fairfords® is a registered trademark of Fairfords Group Ltd and its affiliates.

www.ingramcontent.com/pod-product-compliance
Lightning Source LLC
Chambersburg PA
CBHW070425240526

45472CB00020B/1381